God is Waiting
in the World's Yard

By the Same Author

God is Waiting
in the World's Yard

MTC Cronin

PUNCHER & WATTMANN

First published in 2019
Published by Puncher and Wattmann
PO Box 279
Waratah NSW 2298

http://www.puncherandwattmann.com
puncherandwattmann@bigpond.com

National Library of Australia
Cataloguing-in-Publication entry:
Cronin, MTC
God is Waiting in the World's Yard
ISBN 9781925780062
I. Title.
A821.3

Cover design by The Baby Jesus; Cover art Ulisse Aldrovandi (1522–1605)
Printed by Lightning Source International

This project has been assisted by the Australian Government through the Australia Council, its arts funding and advisory body.

"Become fully, fully yourself in the time
that God gave you."

Bernhard Grossfeld

Contents

Sitting Worldside

Sitting worldside your soulchat
is all about a sleeping kitten,
that is,
life twitches

You are stars and clouds
You flood the same

You are showmen
looking through the window in the mirror
and seeing yourselves
climb back in

The dead bite your ankles
and scream for scraps

But when God drops you
and your worst enemy from different heights
you both hit the ground
at the same time

Sitting worldside your thoughts
are overrunning existence

Life twitches,
that is,
your soul talks between
the dog and gull in the distance

The World's Yard

Right at the back of the world's yard I am sitting. The grave
I have just finished digging is filled by me because the corpse
in it can't do anything. There is a little hymn in the trees
that takes itself seriously though goes completely unnoticed
by the child in the swing. She, or maybe he, has closed eyes
and feet that point. The sun blinks in time with the creak
of the wooden seat. Deadly sins are committed to bird-song.

Downpayment on a Catastrophe

First they are described into immorality. At this point their future guilt or innocence becomes pivotal. The streets become witch-ridden, the parlours full of mutual friends with wooden teeth. Ash comes straight through the ceilings. In every copse the birds get their nibs caught in the bark. But it is engineered! The trick prattles through them, their smiles take a ride on a rattling train. At the bank the one carrying the cash speaks words at their spongy best. "The heart is a rudimentary organ. It runs on blood money." A small black cat wakes in the box in which it was carried to a dump and makes its way home through the drains. The only change in the divine realm is that there is no longer anyone or anything guarding the gates of the dead.

The World's Yard

Right at the back of the world's yard I am sitting. Playing the soul off against three wishes. Cactus. Cactus. Cactus. I am wearing my grasshopper hat. This is a hat in which you view grasshoppers. I read my viewing instructions from a papyrus scented with rosemary. A little group of pretty-shaped stones are jostling at my feet. They bark like puppies. Bump. Bump. Bump. And suddenly, a stem bursts into flower under my hat! I probably believe in God!!

God, the Idea We Had One Day …

One day, between eating, cheating and speaking, I had
the idea. I hurt and I can't feel it. My memory is hurt and
my blood has run from my body and dried. I have a big
fat appointment and I am locked in a room. My eyes are
lower than the grass but in whose eyes does anyone look?
Seven men and then seven boys push a stick through the
gauze of my face and a woman with a million things to do
decides she won't do me. I am lonely. This bites me on the
bum. Sweat drips from my fingertips. My knees are hurting
from being down on the floor. Horizontal cross-pollination.
People pin me to the darkness. My brain flattens their
batteries. The ones that run their hearts and their tides. I
am a beacon, a giant tongue. I'm like a fire on the beach
and by my light you can see the world running round and
round a bush. All fall down! Three-night crawl to a hut to
watch a juggler who tosses then swallows an eyeball with
stitches. Then I get in my car, they get in their cars, and we
drive until we come to a wall that stops us. This all ends in
God. It is pretty obvious to everyone why.

The World's Yard

Right at the back of the world's yard I am sitting. No-one knows I'm here and the world says I can stay as long as I like. If, under my breath, I whisper some response, now and again trees break their postures to eavesdrop but catch only a hint of the lilacs. A large hurricane hits near the fence and destroys a picnic. My heart casts its shadow on the western wall. It seems the ants crawling over it have learnt to speak.

The Evolution of God

God evolved from the tension in the I. From a little bit
of respectableness. There was a red flashing image—
perhaps a word—then dissimilitude and dissemblance.
After this came protocol and after protocol, recognition of
the misshapen creature. (Though it should live it is not
counted as one of the children.) Phenomena now had a
link between each. God could be represented in different
ways. Vast in the midst. A pot-pourri. A vowel-point or a
large vertical fishing-net whose ends are brought together
and hauled. A less usual form of advantage. The evolution
of God goes on. And on. Becoming. All things to all men.
A valve. Roasted fungi to the hungry thing rattling the
bushel. A terrible state; shafts resting on trestles. The
extent to which a thing varies—for example, the whole of
creation—is only where God rests from evolving. Usually
God exploits this coffee break to destroy what is beautiful.

The World's Yard

Right at the back of the world's yard I am sitting. As all reasonable men do. Even more reasonably, though some might find this flagrantly strange, I do not repay insults blow by blow nor by force recover my stolen property. Passing lightly beneath the circus overhead I keep a courtship eye on those around me who believe the world is no bigger than a map. I know how much room there is and that they might need to be escorted in.

God Taste in People

Like lips to the dark taste of milk, I feel God begin to suck
on me. Love, pulled down over my eyes, makes more than
the world disappear. There is no bite of the cherry. No *auris
interna* suffused with cuntroom talk. Yet all is the body.
Submissive Indian, Chinese, Jewish, Greek and Roman, I
am almost too human. I am open. Breast to broken breast,
the morning birds slam into the window of my heart.

The World's Yard

Right at the back of the world's yard I am sitting. Today I am trying the bottom-up approach. My eyes focus sharply on a major danger that lies in the rampant relativism around me. Someone says an eye for a tooth and I don't have a claw. It is clear they are using money for punishment. All around me are uniforms, costumes, badges and flags. One man smiles but it is not clear if he is a forger or embarrassed friend.

Mask of Us

Need, mask of us, worn when we wear any mask, is the only mask with its own eyes. Some violence is required to remove it. Once the face is revealed it is everyone's. (Of necessity, there is no more dependence on freedom.)

The World's Yard

Right at the back of the world's yard I am sitting. I have come here to escape a life. The orchestra has come too. It plays as though Gluck has a humour all its own. (Or at least sounds as though it does.) And there is the town hall trying to force itself through the narrow gate. Its Board of Select Men has put everyone's dreams on hold during the operation that might be an arrival or a departure. The cemetery is recycling the unused dead.

New God

A little bit of trivia from this morning's French news: there is a new god. This god is going to try to be perfect. The old one was. We shall have more faith in this new god because it tries. The old one didn't try at all. Like a sullen child seeking indemnity against failure and the disappointment of all those watching. Those with vested interests. So, what's in the bulletin? The new god has been bred to brave the elements. Self-made ones. The new god can do a cartwheel into the surf and can squat like a baby elephant under something much larger than itself. The new god is a salsa addict and follows the buzz. It's a god that has everything in between, though you might ask, Why the French? The home of *foie gras* and black truffles is the first to discover this god because the inhabitants have been reared on stiff walks and know there is much more to savour in life than food and churches. *Aide-toi, le ciel t'aidera.*[1]

The World's Yard

Right at the back of the world's yard I am sitting. Thinking about ... Leaping eating scooping out the flesh of play. Sublimating exalting purifying venerating ... Could be something to do today. Or I could just sit here and count the suns, watch the old men exercise, cushioned by grass, or the kids pounding the bridge and screaming at the devils as they cross ... Moving these ideas closer is like pushing two beds together. Uncomfortable, I fall down the crack ...

Complainer & Prophet

Like Wallace Steven's poet, being complainer and prophet
and never of the world in which he lives[2] ("Prophets
proverbially getting more of a raw deal in their own
countries than elsewhere … "[3]), there are two beds in
which we sleep, potential and flesh; medium holding us as
if we might wake, a shape; matter beneath the serial bones
of our spines as if to support a dream … Rubbing a fox the
x comes off; forseeing's squished like "riding bitch" …

The World's Yard

Right at the back of the world's yard I am sitting. Hearing sunlight cry out in sleep. The volcano sits and waits to speak. I know how the wind was blowing a million years past. The seabed tells me. I know the volcano has plenty of gods. The seabed tells me, your new god will make your boats disappear. Meanwhile, finding itself in the world, time heals. All night is never all night. Dawn ends. The bottomless present shines.

The God Hand

Nailed to your knees the god hand treats your arms like graced and hungry servants. No other way but in horror. That's what joy is. Life disguised as apocalypse and death as no definite form.

The World's Yard

Right at the back of the world's yard I am sitting. I have lost a circle. Dusk and dawn do not parse. The seasons of my matchless kingdom keep each to themselves. Here the blood's curfew and there the compost sweet as cumquat. Slow realities and lonely realities sit like unyielding seeds in the toothless earth. When I'm alive I feel as if I know when someone is dead. When I'm dead it is very difficult to know if anyone is alive. The life outside life was in the circle.

"The Husband-Who-Hid-God"

The husband who hid god[4] stands next to a rock. His wife lifts it and crawls underneath. The man walks away but the wife doesn't see him go. A flock of dragonflies hovers in the sky's birded song. A new man comes along. Silverly, through a trembling lake, the moon utters a phrase missing more than it can say. The man's woman begins hearing silence. Beyond its clarity a billion trillion things are a very small number involved in working on what's next.

The World's Yard

Right at the back of the world's yard I am sitting. My spine against the spine of a bush. My dictionary open at a word haggling with meaning. At my feet the nodding greenhood orchid, head down as if looking into a black pool and unable to lift its gaze from the sorrow of it. Its reflection, the dark referee, asks is there more past or more future and is answered by a sign from the sign. Eternity never tires of announcing itself in a child's voice.

Statistics (in the Dark West)

Facing toward the altar of their god, back to the dimness,
they give thanks for their personal good fortune. Eagerly,
they think of the morning. When that comes round, the
lizard will not be poking his nose out until the sun is
overhead and his rock well heated. Then he will creep up
and have a good bake. A new day means lots of work for
some people. Also the usual pleasure, pain and idleness.
Meanwhile, the west is dark and the statistics solid as the
lizard's stone.

The World's Yard

Right at the back of the world's yard I am sitting. Approaching along the eighty-year-old branch is an insect with a golden eye. Mud volcanoes erupt periodically. I am studying astronomy as it occurs in the grass. Between the blades, soldiers sent out to test the feelings of the angry. Addictions, feuding and abuse. A headless shifting crisis played out in the tiny jungle of the feet. The world never safe from being about to be formed.

Not What God Intended

God says "It's a little bit them. Not what I intended. I had a thought, an idea. Forgetting that thought may have changed my life. But I went ahead. The pagans were on purpose. Not so the plateaus of desire where people trap themselves. And it appears they have made of my history a treaty of anecdotes. They seem to think. They have done nothing about power. I worked and worked. Now I look and I think *It's a little bit them. But I did not intend them to place all their emphasis on belief.*"

The World's Yard

Right at the back of the world's yard I am sitting. As soon as we finish our tea we can get back under the table. The paint has dried on the bull and tomorrow we'll give him a 2nd coat. He snorts from his yoga position as we hunker down and dread the morn. It's obvious he's cross at our use of wood oil on one of God's most impressive pizzles but from our shared balcony we see a world that's better off maintained.

Sleep-Spot

I have a feeling God is not God. A dog circles its sleep-spot
and falls. The master calls and four paws twitch in time.
God shifts position easier in men than in dreams.

The World's Yard

Right at the back of the world's yard I am sitting. Wearing so many shadows that I am mistaken for night. A skyscraper dreams of the street and men on death row of being boys with sticks in their hands. They follow the tracks of spiders and bury the sticks deep in the bodies of dead rats. Each pretending jurisdiction over the fate of the corpse. Their slumber is broken by freedom making a distinct sound—the earth's crust moving position.

The Caravan on Its Way

Your hands, already, finding ruin. Moving your yard to where the drums are. Your house, alone, surrounded by new trees; flowers now blooming in the dark of your own body. If you listen there you can hear the whispers of those who came between themselves and the light: *Pass by here. Take yourself if you go.* Join the caravan on its way. It is the shape of death. It is shaped like the cities that evicted your souls.

The World's Yard

Right at the back of the world's yard I am sitting. Reading
what is written in smoke across the exhausted air. H E L P
Each letter a single mourner perched, alone, in a bucket in an
endless procession of buckets on a wheel. Impossible to verify
what it cries out for. A record of improvisation? My reading
opens the closed and closes the open. The wheel moves and
the face of an idea turns from the world. Its impossible self.

Who on Earth

The throat of a bird is a machinegun-fired-from-the-shoulder. As it splinters, the door to my skull paints itself red. Surgeons arrive with matchsticks. Hammering them in, they push their noses to the seam of the world in an effort to coax something out of the box. There's no weather in there so they set up a bureau and soon catastrophes are falling to earth. Bad enough, but who on earth is in control of Heaven??

The World's Yard

Right at the back of the world's yard I am sitting. The lamb has a gun. Mother is engaged in removing a stain from the wolf suit. Father has gone to clock his acute soul in. The children have learnt to slander and count their words like sheep. The lamb takes aim. Baby sleeps in the target. She moves her mouth around the dream of a dangerous and divine imprisonment. Mother flinches at the wolf's every bite. Father sells the devil his breath in a bag.

The Sleep of God

In chains made of us, faith is sinking as deep as the sleep of God. Resigned to their hearts, women dream, men are graves. Their thinking resembles the inside of a plum. As if they had been hanging upside-down for an hour and collecting blood in their heads. Nothing can rouse them. Not even a bomb living life to the hilt. Not the statue of a feather falling in the square. Not the screams of children. Not their laughter. Nor even, it is certain, a thimbleful of water tossed by God. In their dreams and graves the men and women die and dream as if they were only sleeping and as if they were dead. Like weather-resistant doormats, their thinking resembles nothing they can believe.

The World's Yard

Right at the back of the world's yard I am sitting. In front of me a stage has been erected over which hangs a sign reading "Houdini Divine". The curtain rolls aside. Upside-down in a glass case of water God tries to look like it's a matter of life and death. But the audience isn't impressed. God doesn't have to get out on time and they know it. This doesn't, however, lead to any complaints out of the ordinary. People always want their money back.

Basic Overview About Approaching Form

How I fact. Believe not believing. Literary but, but social. Chaos plus x. Fear-tone then end-making. By the shove spirit, all faith's claims, games, until only—seems it yet—torturing a brick to find the house. Content is form's ancestry. Form thought it. Two facts in one, divine imprisonment! How forth to the subject ---------------almost there is God.

The World's Yard

Right at the back of the world's yard I am sitting. From my vantage I can see behind journeys where the living step like paperweights looking for Pierre. (How many Peters are walking?) The gears of fiction are stuck. That is why they keep dreaming of moving. They come upon the manshaft and batten it against God's eye where evening blazes. Bored in the womb time wakes. Peter says, *Don't you think I'm always trembling?*

The Bedlam (of Potatoes)

There is a blind species that cannot see the angels. It has
eyes but they are inside the snow or completely dusted
with pollen or merely the after-effect of eyes. Around these
creatures the angels relax like crows with undiscovered car-
rion or an enormous patient volcano dreaming of lichen
and spores. Are you beginning to know the little tin soldiers
who fall to the ground by the wildflower? They have fought
and fought for the hand they cannot see and when scooped
up by the angels are, without refusal, unresurrected.

The World's Yard

Right at the back of the world's yard I am sitting. History is coming up the path with a new appointment in its diary. All the people are in forms that can only shatter or run. Civilization's psellism has them convinced. They mimic sausagy opportunities & sausagy potential. Sausagy ambitions & sausagy outcomes. There are no longer any human splinters to cause irritation to the culture. Belonging-peddler!

The Brunt of God

We have to bear this. Believers and non-believers alike.
Brunts do not distinguish. Single-minded they push you
down. The dark ages come and go depending on who's in
charge of the lights. The resurrectionists say upsadaisy.
The lapsed reincarnationists stamp ants but are secretly
trepidatious and before you can say "you're a gnat" have
relapsed into reimagining their lives as flies. A brunt is
enlarged. It is a feeder. The brunt is a puppet show in
which the puppeteer remains visible throughout the
performance. There are no side seats to the brunt. The
body so selected. For the undeserved mercy of God. We
have to bear this. The short and the long of it. You can
clench your whole body and it will not help. The message
of the brunt is that the ball is at your feet. You are the part
of the horse in front of its rider. A pastime. Do not try to
avoid the brunt of God because then the brunt will begin
to utter poetry. This is pretty but painful and poignant
for the bearer of the brunt. A brunt is like three lots of
Wittgenstein plus more. It is a genius that knows only your
name.

The World's Yard

Right at the back of the world's yard I am sitting. A tree holds the ground in its strong hand. Around it humans are breakfasting and above it are enough birds to move the sky sideways. Today's excitement is that the black swan which was never there is here. It has been picked up on a scanner after years of failure with the metal detector. It reminds me of the lighthouse looking for hidden sorrows and that the time of men seeing with their own eyes has passed.

They Go into Houses

They go into houses, bickering like cats and dogs,
grumbling like an evicted man chewing candles with old
teeth. They lie on beds and stretch their skins over the
scaffolds of their desire, call to the furniture at midnight.
They bury themselves between each other's thighs and
listen for the sniff at the door, rooting out the rotten smell
of the world. They dream on their knees of capturing the
sun like dew but when their shadows turn to mud nostalgia
creeps down to sit in their shade. They wake when they
remember the dawn. They dress in human error. They
go out of their houses, rasping with the organs that have
replaced their tongues, just one long heated howl that will
never succumb to time.

The World's Yard

Right at the back of the world's yard I am sitting. There's been thirty years' war. It's a mediocre time we all share. The sun is the sun and the moon is the moon. The moon of the sea and waterholes has not been seen around here. The sun the beloveds would climb to warm themselves has not been seen. Laughter turning itself over in the sun and that person, so forgetful of themselves because of the moon's light, have not been seen. The war has replaced us. *IMAGE.*

"The Mark Wears Blue / I have Walked for Miles"

Why in every image are there always two women—one who sleeps and one who watches? There is space in images for what the eye cannot see—a distant bridge of reeds, fear whispering behind curtains of redemption. Why in every word are there always two women—one who smiles and one who frowns? There is room in words for the greatly injured, twisted hands, the tiniest operation, a sunny day at the end of Winter. But things are not in words or images. Knock knock turtle shell! Lift the swish of the skirt! Why are there always two women—one who holds, one who lets go? The mark responds in a blue voice: *I have walked for miles in a white dress. The mark wears blue. The Lord has passed away.*

The World's Yard

Right at the back of the world's yard I am sitting. Near me, a man and a woman are crying. She, a body falling past a bridge. He pulling down the world to cover his knives. Grazing her belly—the detour from love to lust. Desire shifting from tongue to teeth. The scar above his temple measured between her two thumbs. Flesh dragging itself, history to solitary history. The public sheds its clothing. He puts his cock in her god. And it crows. Betrayal again.

God-Caused (Carried Away)

From haunch to haunch. From jaw to buttock. A curving
line of ecstasy and freedom. This is not my imagination
but the shape of the Arab's mouth on my mouth. I breathe
the dark green earth. A new sun and a new lake. I lie
in the long grass of his dream and listen to the kiss of
the kingdoms. From maul to maul. From buttock to jaw.
Creatures one on another god-caused with whim and
notion. I take his mouth in my light blue breath—treasure-
that-never-was. His unquiet heart he leaves for me to carry
away on my fingertips.

The World's Yard

Right at the back of the world's yard I am sitting. Guts of the
resurrection spilled at my feet. Having tempted flesh from
flesh in an ongoing Armageddon, time passes and does not pass.
Overhead, a small face, fearful against the plane's window,
sees forever the small boats on their untending sea. A light
green moth lands in the centre of a prayer. I dare, as an atheist,
to mention God and from a wound in my side, sand pours.

Hints

Faith applies only to those with the potential to create gods. Once created, God can make you believe anything.

The World's Yard

Right at the back of the world's yard I am sitting. I have
nothing. I had a stone but lent it to the poet to put in his
shoe. No sooner did he turn into a slim golden feather that
flew straight to the sun that fed the snakes new skins. It
could as easily have resulted in ripe figs resting in baskets
or unruly persimmon trees twirling in fogged mountains.
Regardless, I have nothing. I had a stone but it was just
an essay I wrote once about staying with one's shadow.

God's Gift

The word "god" is a shortened form of lover. It is a
Japanese paper which comes—rolled like a poem—in the
Summer months. Fine and soft. Mulberry bark. The wind
that blows from the mouths of those in love when they
speak is the scent of green lilies bursting from the genitals
of god's desire.

The World's Yard

Right at the back of the world's yard I am sitting. On
my lap, book opened against the complaints of its spine.
It has as the title of love a name. (You can muse on the
different ways of punctuating this sentence, but it is—
quite successfully—striving against punctuation.) I read
aloud and it reads like the rose, its thorn the arrow, drawing
through the heart the lightest and sharpest plough. Between
its lines I'm planted—the outspread white wings of space.

God Can't ...

God can't read. That's why he makes things. He makes
my shirt so that up my sleeve my wives can argue over the
roast potatoes. He makes my ears so that I can hear a man
tired of being said. He makes the ruse to deliver God's
messages and makes the atheist to mention his name.
He makes a head to lick and a chest to rot and upon each
grave a grave. And yes, punishments and rewards. And
yes, the pens and swords with which we fashion worlds to
fall through the gaps in our understanding. He makes the
gaps! He makes an opening in the farce and thighs which
close. Miraculously, without being able to read, he makes us
make names for things which then overflowing like a name
overflow from their names. God is a maker. Skip and a hop.
Striding along like a holiday he makes so much fun that we
feel eternally left behind. We keep writing about it but God
can't ...

The World's Yard

Right at the back of the world's yard I am sitting. Two
women in the seats next to me are sharing a crossword.
The fool climbs out of their lungs with a bagful of words.
Lorica. Gregale. Tepidaria. Sudarium. They scribble and
scratch. Down & across. Across & down. They float out as
if collecting rusty texts from drifting timber, then paddle
back in to pick up their pens. Tesserae! Lapilli! Finally
giving in, I grab their newspaper and set fire to nihilism.

Plus God

Eventually, I let God in. As they say you should. Nothing
changed except that I now had everything *plus* God.
He sat in my priority seating area with a little torch.
Look there! he pointed. A stadium of people emptying a
word. And there! A blue figure in a darkroom developing
extinction, rummaging in itself for the blackness that can
hold up against God's tiny flashlight. And then, well, the
battery goes flat and God and I can see nothing. This is
advantageous because momentarily undistracted we can
really get to know each other. It seems God is interested in
everything about me. This is really nice considering there
isn't anything about me that God doesn't already know. We
talk until the battery shop opens when God can again shine
his little light right at me. I let you out, to go free, he said,
so that I could be everything *plus* you. In the cure of our
equation, it seems, there are no minuses.

The World's Yard

Right at the back of the world's yard I am sitting. The door to the yard swings open—Flowers glitter in small cloths of light—A butterfly is mistaken for one of the tiny red and blue birds that travel the fence in pairs and all around me castles have lain themselves in the furrows that form when history emerges from castles. Their ruins are warmed by the sun, daily intruder into love's brightness. Undisturbed, thorns flaunt the garden.

You are Without an Angel

You just read what you wanted to read. You are always slipping into something more comfortable. You are without an angel. Using your own eyes you can't see anything. You go shopping and fall in love. You fall from the ground. You hurt but you can't feel it. You drag faith. You have a weakness for god. You touch him and think you know what it feels like to survive. You have small words with which you spin a hand and depart your future. Appetite of all definitions, your anguish congeals about your lips while you hide your teeth, at work behind the carcass. You just say what you wanted to say while you devour the present and bid again for tomorrow. See the path become dark. Where the light travels to obscure everything in the precise appearance of itself, see the path become dark.

The World's Yard

Right at the back of the world's yard I am sitting. In my pocket is the shopping list for a dead man. The blindfold I am wearing is a gift that put an end to any reason for which it might have been given. Behind it I contemplate stopping before I stop. Glorious mu. I make a note in my mind to rewrite history from this point forward. Memory finally new, every child in me loses its reason to be born. I'll keep my resurrection to myself.

"Address"

"What you call God, I call out to you."

The World's Yard

Right at the back of the world's yard I am sitting. The only place the wind comes and stays. What ambition do you think the wind has? Yet it carries the dreams of men. And there, the tree, kingly connoisseur of the birds, always happy with daylight as it is. Its leaves, like rain, fit where they fall. And the lake, meeting the land, knows what the cloud says: *My soul dances with my other souls. And yes, they do not exist as I don't.*[5]

Nothing Sits Between God and the Animated

Nothing sits between God and the animated. Ask those who can command a stone. Ask those who die for stones. Ask the chicken living in a field of stones where she lays unbreakable eggs. The stone mind goes looking for stones everywhere. You should know what is between God and a stone. Fog does not sit in the valley forever ...

The World's Yard

Right at the back of the world's yard I am sitting. It would appear it is a world without exception. All of those little black ants. All called George. All doing just what Georges do. Every one poor. Every one knowing how to fight. All with stripes. All with spots. Watch them smile and grimace. Civilizing their epidermis. Stripping their accessory calyx. Tap with your question on their little heads: *Might hunger and cold be indispensable to the universe?*

The One God Out of the Million Gods Who is the God Who Made Us and Does Not Protect Us

This god is the exception. To the stale million. To the alliances between mysteries. To luck. To all those who dance at the dancehall. And it would seem, as we learn to walk, slipping and falling, that this god does not protect us. It would be very nice to choose another god from the possible gods. The little red god. The god who can shield you from the stranger's free will. The god of rotten boroughs. The one who is good company. But we stick with our god as if we cannot step around our own shit. We join with him in the cult of humanity. We swap heads. And he exploits us, prophets and saints in the emptiness of the world.[6]

The World's Yard

Right at the back of the world's yard I am sitting. Holding a fluttering rock and still egg. Hatches battened. The moon is a pretty useless salve for what has most people here hiding under their beds or scrambling into the womb but I'm convinced that if you look into the eyes of the dying you can see death alive. Any legends around confess that they can't stop tinkering with my idea. Meaning doesn't bother. God has a puzzle on the go.

God Has a Stroke

No prettier than the rest of what we've witnessed. God did
it right in front of us. No doubt trying to set an example.
Boozy, muzzy, woozy. Fou as a wulk. That's what the
untrained thought, anyway. We, however, with a bit of
experience in these things, knew right away. There was
some kind of major blockage. A blockage between lover
and slut. Another between the brain and tongue caused
by all those who say God too often (more than once is
often enough to get things clogging). Pile-ups of wishes.
Ugly and hard on God. (Can't speak. Can't think straight.
Rocks backwards and forwards, doing little else without
encouragement.) One woman who'd been through it all
with her mother offered phone numbers. She was outvoted.
Most wanted to have a go at caring for God themselves. As
you can imagine, God has been suffering ever since.

The World's Yard

Right at the back of the world's yard I am sitting. All things simultaneously necessary to each other?[7] Under the microscope a blood cell is lonely. From the cathedral in my chest strangers flow, rechristening the street. Outside the factory they are burning tar barrels for luck. On all the stages their fat tongues dance. In the highest offices they are averaging the dead so that they do not compete for resurrection. One extra thing is godless.

Simple

"[A]s simple and as little ecstatic as possible"[8] I tap my
pencil on a blank pad. I know what matters now. The
bottom line *is* everything. If you think you can't get any
further than ideas of ideas of ideas, it's time to restart your
soul.

The World's Yard

Right at the back of the world's yard I am sitting. A little goose snaps at my arms and a shrub dusts me with the scent of its claims. Over where there seems to be a lot going on, my very own detective is jostling facts to line me up as one. This is worth resisting but I am caught up in the highlife of flies gathering to do justice to the faeces of so much overlapping life. I scream and bite at my own arms but the shrub and duck insist I'm managing.

The Antidote to the Antidote

After taking the antidote to the antidote I know that any
character is worth knowing more about, that everyone
carries a god in their cross-wind. And there in the corner
I find nothing more natural than the corner: just like a
Russian woman kissing my palm and lapping up sobs. Like
a nightwatchman with a breaking moon in his pocket I buy
ticket after ticket in the lotteries of the stars and with every
win propose a toast to the hunter in the special madness
of his boots. It becomes clear, like the crystal that shatters
before the simile, that a rumour says how words will not
unite with things, that justification is the veil for its own
face, that my proof—a personal one—is the counting of
the dead. After taking the antidote to the antidote my spirit
closes itself before the book of prayers and all my laughter
is tears losing their step on the joke. All truth is used and
the clouds move past and the clouds take their place.

The World's Yard

Right at the back of the world's yard I am sitting. Behind
my back the river flows. If I turn to face it it flows behind
my back. I walk away leaving the statue in the garden. I
wonder why it doesn't float out to sea. Wearing God's toes
I walk among the silver hairs of the shivering delta. I
speak to men who are cold and to burning women in the
door-frames of dwelling. They ask for the freedom to make
myths. As if any phrase could do what it liked.

The Scribe Of Small Wonders

The scribe of small wonders with the script of the
particular moment writes. In a room in which there
was never any writing. Hair ungathered at the back of
the neck. Head bent in a cascade of soul. The scribe jots
the indefinite time. So many small wonders adapted so
specially to the smallest star. Recording the form of the
almost complete. Warning all at the entrance to devotion
('It is for the wretch's interest'): *I am the protector of
the throwaway note, of the perfection that falls short of
perfection; I am tracing, in poetry, the outline that is not
there.*

The World's Yard

Right at the back of the world's yard I am sitting. My dead friends come with their dogs. I follow them behind the trees. They point out the hole behind the sky; say their dogs dug it. I am startled by the century this takes. And what it means. That no star has a future as a star. I leave them in the trees. In my house is a faltering lamp. A cup of wine warns the light. *I have been digging a hole!* Dead dogs are in the garden that lives. Where a black rose is only its shadow.

Teaspoon

Today I almost slipped entirely out of the ego. Only a slight poignant sucking remained. That ocean of trolls lapping at God's medicinal teaspoon.

The World's Yard

Right at the back of the world's yard I am sitting. With me is a girl who has a face you could live with for twenty or thirty years and a little lion tamed by her hand. A snake sleeps from her belly to her breast and the red flush on her thighs sings the song of death. The fruit at her fingers falls from the tree of her opened legs as she says: *Accompany me, the cave of around here is where we will live. An empty house, dark window, and candle waiting to be lit.*

The Word Fuck Without Warning

Is like a little bit of encouragement. It can have huge consequences. Make people take off all excited and get a lot of work done. The word fuck without warning is sacred. Like a bull with a massive pizzle. And the cows get littler and littler. The smallest dose you need to get going. When the word fuck without warning is said to God, God laughs right from the belly. God occasionally likes the source of danger to shift and knows that vigorousness in speech can never be underestimated. God, in fact, pisses God's pants when hearing the word fuck without warning. Tickled that man is passing his time with as much as can fill the mouth. That God-given opening in the head by which man eats and utters sound. Fuck is a great word. God knows this because God knows everything. Though often used as meaningless qualification it is always to a great extent. As delicate little receptors we humans give "fuck" such a special accent that God cannot but be proud. And God knows why we say it "poetry's hellish bullshit one good way to suffer men love it men stupid as horses cows"[9] because "Alone in the night ... weighed down by this feeling of powerlessness" fuck is throating us hard, simple and quick. It's a word we can feel. It makes our "tongue as raw as a butcheress. As red as a leg of lamb. Its tip becomes a coo-coo bird crying out. Its cock sobs with saliva. Its bottom becomes our goddess and opens like a mouth. We worship it like the sky and venerate it like a fire. We drink from a gash. Spread naked legs. We open them like a book where what we read kills us."[10] Oh Fuck! And God lights a cigarette. Inhalation is a sacrament. In the aftermath we chat and exchange names, dates and interests. Even though God does not exist the room fills with pungent breath. Exhaling is like a little bit of encouragement. The smallest dose you need to get going.

The World's Yard

Right at the back of the world's yard I am sitting. The stars are throwing themselves from the night's diamond bridge. Shoving the mountains aside I see the moon has no home on earth. A bird skims a branch while a small wolf sits, thrilled by the single fact of the "night". Below the lakes the earth pauses. A swan glides between past, present and future, under an arch and into the deep grand silence that empties the world.

Little "God-Facts"

God knows that blasphemy is not possible. It's all chitter-chatter. God speaks softly of us[11] and if we overhear this whispering we say it isn't real. God says, move when love does! Failure to do so may result in a falling out of love for "God fastens the universe in the movement of God".[12] God stays put when love does. God can be killed but not sacrificed. God is missing from every breath that calls his name. God, the eternal concussion, "being improbable, could exist, and ... since He could ... He should be adored."[13]

The World's Yard

Right at the back of the world's yard I am sitting. Off to the left I see souls stacked up with radiation sickness. They dream they are galloping lanterns while their people walk round without the usual restlessness. In their seven-league boots they wander all the way down the hill to the road's bright fork. The background is turned up high but no-one is even worried about the half-life. By the end of the day the tos and fros of existence are all worn out.

Little Hell

Little hell. The same size, *yes just the same size*, as Hell.

The World's Yard

Right at the back of the world's yard I am sitting. An angel wearing pyjamas joins a dragonfly trying to wake a rock asleep in the sand. Apparently there is a revolution that cannot get going because now does not exist. Those who have turned out for it stand hand in hand so their hands are hidden. There is pizza up the road, a storm packed in every heart and people hiding from guns in poems. None of this matters because life can get away with anything.

Even the Dogs Were Crying

A goose under your arm is a miracle in a gooseless world.
So insists evolution and the best that imagination could
produce was humanity. Every animal with an animal head!
Because only language could say it. *Astra castra, numen
lumen.*[14] At the periphery was drawn the line of science.
Beyond which many sad little souls. And the prophets,
again, squatting to piss at darkslashlight. They said we saw
when everything needed to be restored. "Even the dogs
were crying."[15] "Wretched earthworms called men …
Humble yourselves, adore, and be quiet."[16]

The World's Yard

Right at the back of the world's yard I am sitting. God's mother is pruning in the garden. With a click of her tongue she closes her hand around the spare heartbeats of the unborn, crushing in her palm the soft blossoms tossing their heads like first shadows to the ground after showing their faces to the homeless moon. I call her for a glass of lemonade as above me the apples turn blue in the cold heart of the tree.

Filemot & Yaweh

There are many words for God. There is a word for the colour of dead leaf as if all dead leaves were the same colour.

The World's Yard

Right at the back of the world's yard I am sitting. Everyone here is a yardsman. Ripping overgrown dawns out before every night and shovelling Christmases into the new years. Time's furrow grows ever larger around the edges of their violent labour while I, like a dandelion, watch them and shiver. It seems quite plausible that even the smallest peep out of a dandelion could turn their endeavours in my delicate direction. (As the cat pays no attention to God.)

Baptism by Desertion

They were moving their grief around between each other
as if it was glory. Every no they uttered was used to shore
up the wall they built purely for the purpose of having
a door they could lock. What exists listens at its keyhole
beyond which is the room in which the very shape of
absence is found. In there they echo and fake and come up
only with the idea of detour. This they follow from one
borrowing to another, from one revocation to another until
eventually, gloriously, they grieve for what never left them.
The eternal belief in their desertion and the deceptive
permission this gave them.[17]

The World's Yard

Right at the back of the world's yard I am sitting. Happily watching the young woman on the balcony dangling a cigarette and a pink collar. She's calling her cat who's conducting a disloyal reconnaissance near a bunch of birds who've put down their shovels to have a smoke. Upright, black, in work hats, they swivel their eyes around, questioning the capacity of the clock. The girl yells that birds are "so obnoxious". Hostile buildings shape the grey.

The Mark of God

What is a doll like? To a three-and-a-half-year-old: "A doll is like an old saggy thing or a new thing." To a six-year-old: "A doll is like a mini person but it doesn't walk or talk." To a nine-and-a-half-year-old: "A doll is like a girl that's stunned by the image of something." A doll is the real mark of God. What we make of ourselves.

The World's Yard

Right at the back of the world's yard I am sitting. Carnivorous laughter filters through the woods. Their lovely trees stand against the sun like a scream. Hear slavery in our breath, inhaling not for oxygen but to expel the air we husk to dirty ghost. A thunderstorm is drinking the sky upon which is written this list: *slump, omen, negro, ticket, reward, afterwards, bitch, wolf, faith, hooked.* Then lightning, as it comes to art.

A Billion Years

I don't believe in God. Just a billion years of earthquakes.

The World's Yard

Right at the back of the world's yard I am sitting. Around here, where all miracles are lonely miracles, it's easy to bleed to death. But of course that's only some doctor's opinion. There's always an animator or dust control technician who disagrees. Who says, beyond reasonable doubt, we're dealing with something like you're dying but I'm not. What they all say really. I get up to leave telling them I'm getting a job on the trains. Leaving the ocean.

"The Infinite Performances
of God"

Taking place in all that challenges the miracle, the
"infinite performances Of God"[18]: In my camel's tail; in
"that coarse hair/That is barely visible sometimes/On the
left side of the moon's nose"[19]; in men, who away from
their women, dig for salt on the flat plains; in the plunging
duck; in opinion, in judgement, in blame. All occur in what
is believed to exist which once took place in the "Theater
of Freedom"[20] until its ironic closure through freedom
of choice. Now they are performed in what we believe
is a ruse for delivering God's messages. But God doesn't
have any messages. God has only an act, an act which
we enjoy—fooled by a solace that hides reality; or recoil
from—as if the reality revealed by our slender knowledge
is nothing but the rawest of deals. But like devoted fans we
never budge from our seats in God's tricky theatre. Waiting
for imaginative activity, for the greatest fantasy to ever take
shape, all the time oblivious that the infinite performances
of God take place nowhere but in us. Here, where they
begin and where they end is the punishment that is our
reward and the reward that is our punishment. The stage
that God can never leave.

The World's Yard

Right at the back of the world's yard I am sitting. God comes back with the stick I threw about five years ago. There's not much to do but throw it again. Against the wall of a nearby shed a family is playing darts. A wind interferes. Inhabits the darts which veer off with a cohort of tiny leaves. A nudge at my thigh tells me God's returned, a salivary stick at his feet. It's impossible to tell how much time has passed. There's not much to do ...

God's Companion

God never comes alone. To be even more precise, is always brought by someone else. Or at least this is the story you get from those who talk a lot about being God's friend. But God's friend, God's true companion, doesn't take God anywhere. God's companion has an imaginary friend that he can't convince anyone of.

The World's Yard

Right at the back of the world's yard I am sitting. Down from the sky comes a big hand with long fingers and it pulls the strings that yank me out of the path of a bright blue bulldozer. I think nothing of this but a mild curiosity briefly presents itself when seventeen years later the same hand pushes me off a platform and under a train. The universe, it seems, is tireless. Always hijacking the process set in motion with another process set in motion.

Alteration of the Body by God

This is called pain. (Sometimes referred to as the Soul.)
It is God's way of drawing attention to perfection and
imperfection and where they meet. Pain makes us consider
deeply how to approach others. How we might speak
and what we might speak. Pain creates the cry of pain,
the only communication in which we say only ourselves.
This is *called* pain. The alteration of the body by God so
that we understand risk. Without risk there is no consent.
Without consent we are undescribed and thus lost. Pain
is our compass and our map. With it we locate ourselves,
from which follows recognition. Pain provides us with the
possibility of "self-rescue". Pain is a beacon. (Sometimes
referred to as the Soul). It is God's way of taking up
residence in order to protect us. Without it we would be in
danger. There would be no warning. No warning of the
world. The body in pain makes and unmakes the world. It
is "God's most intimate contact with humanity".[21]

The World's Yard

Right at the back of the world's yard I am sitting. With a small green and yellow spider atop the clay flower in the child's noon hand. Why do we always feel like children? Because we only *don't know how to be* children, says the adult I've created. There is also, close by, a little pebble, a tiny cheep, scream of someone small for whom no-one waits. Lungs locked on the deaf air. I could console. Should go. I stay like this.

On Every Doorstep

On every doorstep, in swaddling clothes, a time-bomb
falling out of the womb, destiny found abandoned despite
the histories muttering. "A prize is awarded to a photograph
of two women bringing their children across a swollen river
in war-time." Immaculation has no release, will always be
saying this grief. "Someone will come to help us now. The
churches are made of stone, our bodies changed back to
flesh and blood."

The World's Yard

Right at the back of the world's yard I am sitting. The saints are trashed and have swapped lying down naked next to God[22] for a little hut with the sun streaming in. Likewise, a window has been traded for the horizon it will never meet, a fruitless tree for what grows itself and our future for the breath never wasted. This prompts me to see if anyone will give me the sea for a bottomless photograph, the gun for the curfew or a % for the personality of an accountant.

God is a Survival Instinct

People seem to think God's got something important to
do with them being dead. (If they weren't going to die
I wonder if they'd bother about him at all!). God has a
bit of a giggle at this but, necessarily, gives up the ghost
at life after death. Self-eternity is simply the ongoing
"monotonous suicide of God!"[23] Killing himself laughing
at an outlook seen coming by introspection; hanging on not
to the here-and-now but the idea of it.

The World's Yard

Right at the back of the world's yard I am sitting. It is true here that the hat never lies to the head and the bucket never poisons the well. Still, people love and push each other. It is an everyday thing to take everything from someone. As if you had to be taught that you have nothing. Again everyday. And people hold objects that make them crazy. I can even see a woman hanging on to her last hope which she found near her last chance.

God's Pedigree

God's pedigree is known only to treasure hunters. White foam trays of fish are laid out. The baker has baked too much bread—ask the soup kitchens. Roses on roses on roses ... Nowhere is there artificial light. The same woman is sleeping with everyone. Out on the water are one thousand dancing feet. You are a little map covered in x's. The secret? God is finding himself and that's why you can't.

The World's Yard

Right at the back of the world's yard I am sitting. Violent languages can be heard hissing from a fistful of lips. An empty landmark crawls over to sniff at the steaming soles of my shoes. A man's head blows off. What comes out of the top—coins or ghosts? "It's the existence that determines the chance" screams the big slot-machine that lumbers in from left field. Pushing all its buttons is "the belief that God cannot be 'known' but may be directly experienced".[24]

The Experience of God

The *experience of god* is not fainthearted despite that one may faint. It is like a summary. Hitting your head on a lamp-post or kicking your toe on the leg of a table. Digging a hole that fills another hole. Exoskeleton in a beautiful box. A system of coloured flags that says statistically you haven't a hope and so hope wells up like a glass half full emptying into a glass half empty. After this you have no energy to deny the effects of your beauty. Swooning and falling into the open arms of God, who with the void in his hands, makes you what's left.

The World's Yard

Right at the back of the world's yard I am sitting. One bit of the future is breaking from the present. Hooking the mind with prophecy. Those who are mistaken see this as an opportunity to begin their memoirs. Most simply line up to get old. Habitually ending. What happens, happens, they might be muttering. Like it did when it will. As for me, I balance in the lopsided now and don't allow the stars to begin.

Above Us

Above us we hear the windmill yelping, circling like a
trapped dog while the house sits like a black skull on the
hill. Above us the tombs are rising from their rest and
travelling along the roads beneath trees turning sourly.
Above us the wind flings uncountable seed into the
dignified light tossed through the depths by a green moon
rolling over and over in the shifting lens of the waves.
Above us nakedness stretches forever against danger,
ravishment and smoke. When we wake our lives are on fire.
Above us only our sleepy souls drifting like reeds catching
the air.

The World's Yard

Right at the back of the world's yard I am sitting. The horizon cracks and reignites the fire. At my desk in the garden last night I wrote these words in our ashes: "No honouring. No aligning. No alleviating. No levelling. No rights. No rescuing. No reference. What keeps us together, you have to work out." Now, in the morning, past the ideas of men, a row of small broken windows sits on a shadowed wall with no door. They look how we look.

My Flaws

Undeserted my desert. Unabandoned my abandon. No gifts.
No talents. I am what God understands. Huddled under his
heart without humiliation. My flaws in doubt.

The World's Yard

Right at the back of the world's yard I am sitting. The angels, who initially thought there was no such thing as us, now have dirty fingernails from dealing with us— lots of nights spent sniffing around like improvised dogs; days stalking out ground in advance of our souls. Regal but winged like eagles they've decided, may as well claw what can be clawed. As a tiny challenge, I mouse myself for them, these guardians of the small and the casual.

"Danger-Angel"

Wears steel-capped boots and belts the sky with barbed-wire tipped wings and when danger-angel opens its mouth it usually says things like: God says you can get fucked!

The World's Yard

Right at the back of the world's yard I am sitting. An army is approaching. Out of step for the life of the bridge. Because they thought we needed a bridge—to get from this to that. *This*, because there is a god simply words, and *that* because translated all these words say, "How do you say it?" And so they advance along a long explanation that can bear only a short one: "To get from here to there is the only story on offer." Retreat is my retort.

Strange

The jug of water I left on your step has been found by all the world. How strange, then, that the water from God is in no-one's cup.

The World's Yard

Right at the back of the world's yard I am sitting. Having a cold beer and an argument with my best friend. She says when it comes to art, the only (right) place to be is in the wrong place. I insist on Hell as she takes a swig and shakes her pretty head. Right here right now chickenshit, she says, looking around at the bluebonnets running head to head across the field. "The poet will no longer imitate nature, for he doesn't allow himself the right to plagiarize God."[25]

We Call Them

"What the gravity-agenda scientists need to realize is that 'gravity waves' and 'gravitons' are just secular words for 'God can do whatever He wants.'"[26] Some people do whatever they want. We call them sociopaths.

The World's Yard

Right at the back of the world's yard I am sitting. Every day, the living and the dying, the great switcheroo. Driving with the radio on and then stopping to pray at two little churches side by side. They light candles and then blow them out. Afterwards, it's a little pub for lunch where too much happens between them to ever take it back. After all, life only does up to a certain point and then, half-full, half-empty, glasses raised, *Long live the dead!*

No Resurrection

No resurrection is enough for the living. They think
differently about "skeletons" and "their skeletons".
Dull with premonition they press their flesh against one
another. Caught in the vice of here-and-now, marooned
in the wayside of time, they eat the light, chew the bones
of angels and spit out the moth of night. All is rush and
stillblown. Everything, hoarded for reality as, preferring
faith, dreams go missing. Claimed by earthspace they are
busied, busy funnelling God into the Godspace.

The World's Yard

Right at the back of the world's yard I am sitting. Eyes laked at the bottom with tears, latinly, quickly burning against the world and the windows which pass at night, windows opening both ways on to worlds of similar-sized emptiness that contain nowhere. Fingertips rub the length of a sill, lift, and never part the sky—On the soft green grass birds burst into flight. They think they are entering the ocean but it is my heart. My heart which keeps letting go ...

What the World Tells Us

In a grunt, in terror you cannot come near, it speaks to
us now from its dirty sheets, from its salt mine, from the
dark office where it stays late, scribbling on the walls and
sleeping off the wine. O baby bird, O flower standing alone
in a field, there is no distinction between a fairytale and a
murder. A village is razed by the grass that grows after, the
wind unsearches and the sea unclaims, darkness doesn't
know itself and so remains in darkness. There is no church
in this room, no school, no people except for the automatic
crowd and the guard-hornet who have been waiting for
you. Forever. The world who has been waiting for you
forever. "I am speaking to you now and I have done away
with words. I have set the table for telling. Your hunger is
inspired. Your emptiness is God."

The World's Yard

Right at the back of the world's yard I am sitting. The long-beaked bird questions the tree. How thorough is the world? Why must we keep arguing about what we know? The wildflower and its gallery are silent. I think about when the Greeks got Greek and why in all our hearts history gathers. Around me the sum of existence is wringing its hands. Trying to work out what luck does and trying to work out why it stopped doing it.

God Isn't Dead, Just Indifferent

God didn't intend anything absurd. Not the sasquatch or the French military cap. Not anonymous works or acedia. A bunch of strata heads, a board of select men, the virile magistrate with "an intolerable burden of dealing in inches"[27], the deceased Mrs X and the living Mrs X—God didn't intend any of them. As they are all here, however, God, having not intended them, ignores them. This leads some to believe that God is dead. Proof that he isn't is sometimes based on a lack of proof. In a buggy meant for the moon, God—looking like he's visited a taxidermist— travels from airport to airport. Like Prince William (Windsor) whose "precious memories are of meeting real people with his mother [Princess Diana]",[28] God keeps his eyes open. Problem is, he's a bit like a text—circulating without content, i.e., open to interpretation. But there's only one way to read him. His indifference is because he sees us all for what we are—dead people.

The World's Yard

Right at the back of the world's yard I am sitting. Tables bristle under striped umbrellas. Seated there are the humans. They are being counselled on the limits. With no moorings, they represent actors. In the distance between thinking, their heads bend forward to catch the fragmentary whisper emanating from the whole of the universe: *For things to matter, you need more than one thing.* (Someone should grieve. Every thing is worth that.)

God's Genes

"Everything has genes of God inside."[29] These genes wield the tremendous clout of remorse. Inheriting them means inheriting the game. The need to be an offender. These genes align us with each other so that we may see how to destroy each other. Sweets from a stranger. Kindness of the stranger. The genes of God that are in everything are ritualized, as is the visit of a butterfly to a flower. They give rise to deformity, monstrosity and distinction. They are, themselves, a trauma. An interrogation. From time to time they have no definition and then the song begins. It is a song of pursuit. Sung by the creator and the created. Both pursuing. Both pursued. Genes have no inkling of these finer points. They simply sing along without understanding the words.

The World's Yard

Right at the back of the world's yard I am sitting. Around me the desert looks less like itself than like a simple lack of "landscape"—as if it were the second shadow of itself. Leaking through the rents of a forgotten sea, sand perceives itself as what is wept from the rock. Above me, a sky the colour of felicity is softly tucked as a blanket to its edges. Cities picnic on it, melting one to another. Peering up I marvel at their perseveration, their lofty ambition to perish.

God's Ambition

God's ambition to be God. Our ambition for God to be God?

The World's Yard

Right at the back of the world's yard I am sitting. In a screech, the afternoon takes off. The noise of a machine ceases and, as if relieved, the breeze spills itself into the dry eucalyptus. Six cocky chickens advance. A feral dog yowls like a beautiful woman's hair. The lake dances. Shepherdless. The lake unfurls and is still. Full of upside-down clouds. All summered up. And sun falling through broken windows into half the planet's circumference.

Link

Starred and starred. The lamp dreams. The universe
expands. Death-in-general, the size it is growing into. In
a cave, hearts wait. Quivering. Rabbit-kisses. Love wakes
everything. Flutters. But is the moth light's trophy or is
light what's won? Awake at last to the word of God. *Life is
the weak link.*

The World's Yard

Right at the back of the world's yard I am sitting. Everything around me is made of graves to which life offers everything. In fact there are no years here where years keep passing. Busy. The dog sleeps. Puss-moth and kitten-moth rising spirally to the light. Smaller kindred of the ghosts. Again, dawn transgresses. Rain will fish and kiss the grass. Trees lining up like goddesses. Along time's hidden path I see the birds take their bath in the last of the afternoon.

The Whole World

God says, "Again this week, it is the whole world that
bothers me. I put my hands above my head. I clown. But
my skin gives off no warmth and my ears don't prick. My
thoughts are like the inhabitants of a big country illegally
living in a tiny town where the immigration officer calls
and calls. Someone like an uncle is always complaining and
a cow with an aneurysm is just another example of what
is mistakenly called fate. It really is troubling that this is a
world in which people are required to prove the cause of
death of a testicle, the vas like wet spaghetti. It is seriously
unfortunate that their touchstones are torture, testimony
and tender. Don't they know that each and every one of
them appears to me as a woman sitting in blistering heat
for a bag of flour and a pinch of salt. This is about how
what is doesn't explain why. But no amount of dancing
about like the greatest fantasy to ever take shape is going
to convince them of the truth: That to be human is beyond
God. To live, a temptation."

The World's Yard

Right at the back of the world's yard I am sitting. Many things appear to be dust and reasons for death are many but on this day I see only one bird in the sky, the father and the daughter out walking—she follows his steps as if they are her own small shadows, tender feet falling, arousing the earth. All around them time does its business yet still I would ask, *What is so important about now? Why do we not sense the earth's movement?*

What Are Those Things in There Made of?

Planets? C's? Paperbags? They are certainly not photographs or fleas. The two most stupid people in the world have come to help us work it out. They say they're not a deathhole or keys. We settle on specks. But what are the specks made of? Diadochi? Pogroms? Increased poems speaking with the tongues of the saddest animals? The stupid people don't stay. They must attend a conference on an argument that has already been disposed of. What do you think the things in the specks are made of? We would like an answer that satisfies the conditions under which nothing holds true.

The World's Yard

Right at the back of the world's yard I am sitting. The whole world should stop. But the whole world never stops. The president's restless brother continues being a general flayer among us and a baby is just born and instantly recognized by its mother. Really, everyone in the whole world is either saving the whole world or doing something terrible to their friends, playing with the set of evil and playing with the set of good as in this involuntary game, we sit.

The Occasion of Sin

The train likes the other train and perseveres along this track come hell or high water. This, though, is not the occasion of sin. That is not hanging around long enough to see what happened after the sparks flew. Because of a timetable.

The World's Yard

Right at the back of the world's yard I am sitting. I see
harm get off the train. Warriors of the pen and brain rally
behind thickets of summer grass. They pick a number and
fight over it. Such a taste for screaming. How much death.
And further death. There are no third parties. No more
news of poets and names. Decades pass without a single
scientific exhibit and during which someone boards up the
cubby. Pain is adjusted to the population's special needs.

Is It God?

There is a direction taken by the dark rock in the night.
This direction is the departure that brings you closer to
God. Follow the rock. Be spinning and mute. Without being
able to speak, say of the harmony, It is not God. Say of the
emanating, It is not God. Say of the climax, It is not God.
As the rock wears, listen closely to its grains of truth: There
is a magic axe. It is not God. There are two immortal tigers
mating. They are not God. There is blessing and victory.
Not God. There are directions taken by the sands in the
night. Break yourself and follow them all. Is it God? Is
it God? Is it God? Is it God? Is there no single glory? Is it
ultimately with stillness and silence that the question is
acknowledged as answer?

The World's Yard

Right at the back of the world's yard I am sitting. All around me are hollows and echoes and analogous mislooking. I am holding a tool for nothing. Chipping away. My working notes tell me there is a truth buried in the mountain of compromise upon which we base our common life. Many of those toiling around me believe in craft but I am slowly uncovering the beauteous organization of accident. Oops! Just did it again.

Another Billion Years

Alive with swarming and wine, all-risked, they align
themselves, alert God with their smoke, ask for the
fearful sign and God beats them a billion years ago by not
replying.

The World's Yard

Right at the back of the world's yard I am sitting. Without a trick and at the mercy of common harms. Jokes are doing the usual jumping and my life splits off now and then into my concerns and those same renouncing themselves of their own accord. And all through this little things. As little as the dream suffering in the tip of the little girl's finger as it lifts the leaf. As little as the sandal in the world. We are all defenceless but only because there is nothing to defend.

The God-voice

Shamans whispering into loudspeakers. "At first they existed on the fringes of English departments, which was probably healthy. Without advanced degrees or formal career paths, poets were recognized as special creatures. They were allowed—like aboriginal chieftains visiting an anthropologist's campsite—to behave according to their own laws."30 " 'Speaking in the God-Voice' I heard him call it. 'Of course,' he added, 'if you speak in the God-Voice you say an awful lot of stupid things!' "31 But it's not that I know what to say. I know what to hear. " 'God,' he said, 'is the harrowing reply to the posthumous accusations of Creation.'"[32]

The World's Yard

Right at the back of the world's yard I am sitting. Right outside the front door to my house which is in a dry little town or a town on a lake that threatens to flood. Meanwhile, God has managed location, location, location. Still, I wonder how to find where God lives. How to make God follow me home when God will not be unjoined from God's only kingdom. All day like this until I hear someone calling me in. *Darling, your hot soup of tiny pains* ...[33]

Somewhat More than God

I am making a list "post-god". This includes some things
that are more than God. From a distance it resembles the
small figure of an alpinist who has been identified on high
land; up close, a driveway that can never be parked across.
And just to elaborate, because that all sounds a bit precious
and, additionally, because the list is not readable, included
on the list is how to stand, how to sleep, how to chew. How
to stop and how to be everwhelmed. Despite such clarity,
however, the list is a bit of a riddle. No-one knows if it's a
list of things to do or of things to avoid doing at all costs
and though I have plans to take it shopping it has already
resisted all attempts at uncrumpling. Really, what it is is a
list of things that have been crossed off as they have been
written. A big red line drawn right through each as if taken
down by the universe's most active shooter. What did you
think you were going to do after God. Ambushed like fear
by prayer?

The World's Yard

Right at the back of the world's yard I am sitting. There is news today of casualties. Perhaps they were drinking from the ocean or simply said, sorry, we're alive. Regardless, dead goes straight to it. Driving through as it throws people out the earth-window. I watch it disappear around a bend in the space-time continuum hitting a dog as it goes. Poor thing was playing dead in the wrong place at the wrong time. Nought to be done, I go back to playing alive.

Call My Name

Call my name, God said, and I heard words from some
other him.

The World's Yard

Right at the back of the world's yard I am sitting. Stomach purring. Becoming virgin. Trucking wood through the mountains. Driving to the trees which frame the town. Flying to the ground. I am the ladder that God climbs. Brainstem quivering like a speared fish. The sky is my heart and no bird can leave it. Nothing has ever drowned in me. I attach a petrol-soaked rag to a dart. Being bored as a child is different to being bored as an adult.

The Secret Criminal

The secret criminal could be prevented by neither logic nor conscience, by emotions nor by sanity. Eventually they gave up their life of crime after reflecting on the banality of evil but primarily because they were tickled by God. The only god that real criminals will pay attention to is the god that tickles them.

The World's Yard

Right at the back of the world's yard I am sitting. The yard a corner. The world—how the weight of it in the hand is exactly the difference between what is known and what is directly experienced. In it, the saddest days consisting of imagined sadness and the happiest simply treated like members of the family. Chanting over and over the spell of the landscape and tossing flowers to cause it I wonder what comes next. A monstrous eternity?

What God Didn't Need to Get

Since God got a preventable infectious disease, it's been a culture
in decline. It's been an island. Not a good island. An island of
forced isolation. An island without everything we need. Peace
has been invaded. All the messages sent receive a single reply.
The premier may as well be the president may as well be the
general may as well be the prime minister may as well be the
beetle missing its antennae. Sometimes, in the middle of a
fanfare, someone stands up and screams. Then the grass grows
twice as fast. Someone pours the cement. Then a few more
people decide not to be eaten by the pride of lions they invented
to protect themselves. i.e., they decide not to be eaten when
they should have been. Immediately, this lot become pretenders
and a drain on available services. If only they could take to the
horizon at sea. (They think it is a poem and not something to
worry about!) God is too ill to notice. God waits for a cup of
tea. Paradise wafts around the sick room. (The smell is a bit
lyrical.) But the sea has got rough and no amount of defecation
by God's sea-creatures can calm it down. Here on the island we
are no longer grateful for our quarantine from new (possibly
unknown?) diseases. We understand fiercity. Possibly even how
to restart from the point of being alone. In the early evening,
when the sun melts our resolve, we might make God's soup, but
during the cello playing and the putting out of the compost we
just about ignore God's whole existence. We are determined to
live. We are determined to get off this island of God's sickness.
We blame God for getting what God didn't need to get if God
had been more careful. We sit in committees and discuss this.
If only we could see things more for what they are instead of
noticing at every instant God languishing all around us. If only
God had accepted the immunization. All around us the ocean sits
in its hole but between us all there is not a single boat that floats.

The World's Yard

Right at the back of the world's yard I am sitting. Around me new seeds flicker like fingers uncurling from a dark fist. Children are singing. *The stem in the vase does not reach the stream.* Their parents play on the memory-go-round. Dart like flowerless insects from one of their own sorrows to the next. The true cultivator knows he always tends another's garden. Almost as if they have evolved to leave, people understand so late that it doesn't happen in their lifetime.

God, the Toy

"God is the greatest toy that was ever made, radiant, infinitely large and small, and now He is broken."[34] Now devoid of fundamental analogies I think I'll go play with something else——maybe the mud or my genitals.

The World's Yard

Right at the back of the world's yard I am sitting. Applause comes after the sunset but I will not put my hands together. There are to be no congratulations on making one piece of art. You may as well put your bum in the air or take out your teeth! This general banging around and tying of lassoes and making things pretty is enough to make God faint. It is possible to understand a sunset. And you don't sit there clapping.

Writing God Down

Words. Tapering towards the end of the thing where
they fall off. Write "HOPE". No, that's not right. Write
"MULTIFARIOUSNESS". No, no. Try "MAUVAISE HOUTE".
Closer, but such unjustified shame, such painful diffidence
can never last. Doctors of the Law, Saints and a handful of
great scholars are preparing the divine names and creating
a vocabulary in which to speak them. God has been the
most philanthropic eponym, giving his name to all people
and places. (With some minor slipups: "for example,
there was a big furore in the Japanese government a
while back about the character commonly used to mean
'woman', which is based on a symbol for a person sweeping.
Apparently there are better alternatives they wanted people
to use ... "[35] And then there are the atheists who want to
be able to say the word "God" without being harangued
by believers who say "How dare you, an atheist, mention
God!") But God is the unavoidable text. 'R' might be the
dog letter, trilling on the tip of my tongue but the letter
for god is thrilling. It's all about oath. And how what you
say can kill you. Or how what you read can propel you into
eternal longing. I say God and I say it again. I've said it
before and I'll say it again, I want those beautiful wordsters
to stop breaking my heart.

The World's Yard

Right at the back of the world's yard I am sitting. In the burning pit the bodies co-ordinate their deaths. The sun's gold thread underlines the flame with coloured flags that turn the wind in the direction of a lost circle. The stream runs in the leaves calling them down to where they lose their seeds in a callous valley of ash. One of the bones speaks. None of the bones speak. A breeze raises its voice to compete with the silence.

The Boneheap

Bones that never had any flesh held onto me. Some called it justice, some art. It was what they had to say, they thought. Piled up like what even God would discard.

The World's Yard

Right at the back of the world's yard I am sitting. Everyone is gathered around the thing from her country. It can save people as well as God can and feels like having a twenty-four-hour-a-day-massage. Someone claims it has a nose as sweetly cold as a cat's and others that it gives men a decent reason for killing each other. They say it is pointless to put forward any excuses for which it should not be exported and the only sticking point is its distrust of us all.

God's Girth

According to José Lezama Lima "The girth of God
continues to be of use."[36] I suspect God's girth might be a
bit like *fe fi fo fum*. A litter of pigs or a pod of whales might
suffice on a bad day but what God really wants is *humanity*.
His appetite is whetted by "the bad luck of our not being
God"[37] which makes us smell like a mulberry on an orange
tree or the bare back of a horse newly deserted by the
sweet thighs of a lady. We are delectable and even moreso
when we think God does not exist because we do not know
what God is. God is what devours us as we try to hide in
God's corner. God needs to feed and is lonely only for us. He
has our emptiness by the throat and it tastes like boxloads
on truckloads. As his mouth lets go there is just this whiff
of adoration ...

The World's Yard

Right at the back of the world's yard I am sitting. Eating a French jargonelle pear. A neighbouring sky pours out butterflies. A dizzy rose dances with my soul. The moon's rise is like the glimpse stretched halfway to eternity. Its pheromones tempt the blood from the briar. A ladybird turns over a zebra and looks in its stripes for a night black with sugar. The ants gently lift a new burden while my heart is germinating with all that breaks it.

Auto-da-fé

God comes out onto the stage and asks the same question we've been asking since time began, then corpses (thespian-speak for cracks up laughing). Someone in the audience starts booing and God leaves the stage through a trapdoor in the floor as smoke rises and obscures the backdrop. Someone screams fire. Instant pandemonium. But the theatre has no exit signs and people race around pretty much crazy and bumping into each other in almost complete darkness. Every now and then someone intelligent and brave takes the stage and yells a lot of smart things in an effort to calm things down. Things like "God is only an actor" and "It's a play, it's not real" and "The question was just fiction". No-one listens. God had played the part too well ("to whose mastery belongs knowing how to seem"[38]) and nobody was in the mood for religious deconstruction. The dialogue was the proof. Every single one of them was going to remain in this goddamn burning down building—screaming and climbing over each other, dead or alive—until God rose again through the bloody burning floorboards. (Or at least until they found an answer.) There is no telling how great an impact the dramatic experience can have. The audience becomes the audience. The crowd becomes the crowd. "At the play … each one enjoys possession of all."[39] "The masses are born fire-worshippers."[40]

The World's Yard

Right at the back of the world's yard I am sitting. I listen to a man lamenting the work of the mosquito but catch only a delirious ramble. There are three governments arguing near the fence along what—according to a fractious compass—is the eastern boundary. They remind me of the battle of my outline with the world in the dream I never had where butterflies occupy every interval of air between the trees and their silence.

Types of Souls

There the souls are differentiating themselves. One, the daughter of a billionaire. Another, a nightingale. Gypsies on the city bench. King of the Belgians. If you believe in all these you might believe in anything. Even God! For whose eyes the souls keep insisting I'm a knife or a fork, as if one was a moon and the other the sun. Look, here the souls are differentiating themselves. Nailed to their meated posts. Shaken loose from creation.

The World's Yard

Right at the back of the world's yard I am sitting. My head is empty, my body is light and my chest is clean. I am sheeted for burial. Next door to the asparagus patch. In the anteroom of earth. There, nothing will care less about the many tears wept and the many unwept. There will be for me a dwelling in which I will not dwell, where held down by heavy rocks I will be buried as I buried God in my worship, held by myself underneath myself.

What We Are to God?

Corollaries? Atoms? Frisson? Violence? (Because it's everywhere.) "We are, in fact, his suicide note."[41] (Found when it's too late.)

The World's Yard

Right at the back of the world's yard I am sitting. Near me, a tribe surrounds a man with stars in his thinking cap. It found him crawling, hands full with everything from which it is possible to die. A wind searches for leaves to turn while death settles on his heart like a blanket thrown upon a winter vagrant. With a little bit of relentlessness the tribe lolls there in the arms of the late afternoon, trying to get a grip in life's hollow.

Data

The air smells of vibration. The angel is dancing around
signals. At the observatory this is what they call data.
Outside, the satellite watches. In the corner of its eye the
angel flutters. Would you say it's alive, an angel? A man
records his observations as directions merge. *Clinging to the
east, wings.*

The World's Yard

Right at the back of the world's yard I am sitting. Here, there & everywhere I see people slide off women. They have heartbeats of their own, little minds getting educated in their guts. Not even the busiest angel of the Lord is as busy as them, thrashing away like frogs born out of the pond, in the pond like stones with arms and legs. Their starved species of ecstasy is a frenzied shrieking adoration of "something to do" while licking the dust from nothing.

Yum Yum Yum

All gods are eventually eaten by time. No devil ever tasted
so good. Gods have the rotting dying flavour of living.
Piquant. Poignant. As soon as I finish one I want another.
Luckily history keeps on spitting them out.

The World's Yard

Right at the back of the world's yard I am sitting. This morning I woke with only the bump of my questions in the brightness. What did God make during the day? What at night? What about law? What about a tiger? Are we messy or undefined? Carelessly made? Is God then shoddy? A mindless slob? A bullshitter?[42] In the face of this bullshit should I remain steadfast? There is only the black bump of my question and a triangle no one has ever seen.[43]

Life

An incident in which you are slapped in the face until admitting that you killed God.[44]

The World's Yard

Right at the back of the world's yard I am sitting. On the
lawn some children have a doll. They feed it and save
it from wild animals. Clearly it is a baby and they are its
parents. About halfway through the game they create
karma and then the game never ends because this is
something there is no way out of. An innocent morass
begins to approach the little group which immediately
becomes a tableau of fear. Nothing can join a tableau.

Home

As a definition, it approaches God. Flesh-coloured after
flesh has been growing through four seasons in very rich
soil. Living and dying in the same place. Being patted to
sleep. Bubbles that stay alive is a concept that might drift
through your mind. Put on your name-tag if you don't
want to be a stranger! Earth's on the up—turning like
dreams. You can do no better than put smiles in the mouths
of gods, complain to a fir tree that all you have is trees.

The World's Yard

Right at the back of the world's yard I am sitting. My hand grips the wind. In my line of sight is a poem: *A man walks into a river and does not walk back out. Beneath the waters a sentence drowns.* Sunlight feels just like itself without any exercise of memory or the imagination. A watering can retreats from the garden so as not to be impregnated by a tidal wave while an earthquake hits the chicken coop. The chooks reject "ashes to ashes".

The Lifespan of Faith

A thief has stolen the western wall. Also missing is the war that was going on for around eighty-six years and a poem that was doing very well (being on its way to the next one). We try to speak of what is not going on but our words dumbly stand in for our thoughts until we can no longer think them. Very soon there is no more to do than descend to our haunches, *telos* broken as its promise, and unwait. We do not know (and nor can we believe) if we do this together or alone. Each of us is hidden from himself by himself. For the lifespan of faith.

The World's Yard

Right at the back of the world's yard I am sitting. I wriggle a little in my seat and the divine settles down. Cutting one's bum on a thistle is not an option and nor is waking the mother bear. Startling an overtired sniper, the flickering oak next to me apologizes and resumes the day before yesterday. Life is a haze of waiting and occasionally a dream rises from it. My arm on the window of a car, forgetting steering and growing warm in the sun's mouth.

God-Only-Knows

What nobody mentioned. That not everything is
represented. What underpins the example. That being God
commits a genetic heresy. What an accident misplaces.
That sin is itinerant. What is necessary. That a friendship
with God always mimics the truth. What the appearance
of things is for. That difficulty is as simple and boring
as a schedule. What God's anecdote about the end of the
universe does to the historical development of the joke.
That judgement is a resort. What the dream distinguishes
between. That sleep is not over.

The World's Yard

Right at the back of the world's yard I am sitting. Note of a small bird dies & rises. Cumbent sun & moon marrying the sea. Grandeur containing a winding stair. Nature kissing in a knot of wood. Under my straw hat a little ode tugs at my lips, follows the dip & up of wings along the fence tips. Ferns sail past palings over which peeps a gent in a crisp white shirt. Raising his little silver-birch baton, the bird's throat opens as if it were the door of the composer's house<

Knocking on Your Door

Inhabitants? What are you in the moon? Little man or little woman thinking how to rest or run. When the suns are counted what will be left to divide up with your hands? She was breaking bread and he was describing it as if it was an old story when they stopped to listen. Is that God, the wind we hear coming? God, what we breathe from bent double? God the fire we taper off? God the earth now cracking, once everything the foot desired? Curiously, surrounded, they act as if they can hide, as all humans have always hidden from God. Trembling. Questioning. Is that God's step crushing the stair. God's screaming, *Inhabitants, who lives here?* Little man, little woman, unable to rest or run. It is done. Knocking on your door is the knocking on your door.

The World's Yard

Right at the back of the world's yard I am sitting. Looking.
We are all spectators with nothing to do with it. This place
with a lot going on. There is terror. There is alarm at wildness.
There are cures and curses. There is experience so terrible.
Over the back is a pile of words rotting and right here singing
that softly covers everything. Seems the end is nigh. On a
headstone, finch leads the way. Soaring song. Upstaging death.

The Deep Cloud of Human Curiosity

Do you think God knows what we're doing when we create God? Do you think God sees everything, even the big obvious god? Do you think God exists like idle speculation? Do you think God cares more than your mum? Do you think God will save you from doctrinal solipsism? Do you love God more than you question? Do you think God knows what we're doing? (Curiosity cannot exist outside an obscuring cloud. If you need to ask, you cannot know.)

The World's Yard

Right at the back of the world's yard I am sitting. Angels are urinating on the grief we never get any better at. They've been apprised but always forget to suffer. Where they pee saffron changes colour one hundred times in a poem. The sun loves it because the sun is in love with our death. I just think: *To lie in a field with a dog.* But the field is roaring not with the field's voice. Alongside it the river confronts the veins of our hands—they do not pray.

God Creates the World with a
Golden Circle from the Chaos

"God creates the world with a golden circle from the chaos."[45] Like an expert tracker, God widens and widens the circle until its circumference fits over the edge of being. Then God locks it. With us inside. With all of creation inside. Nietzsche rushes up and breaks his nose on it. From his bloody handkerchief mutters *"Around the hero everything becomes a tragedy, around the demi-god a satyr-play; and around God everything becomes—what? Perhaps a 'world'?,—"*[46] Wittgenstein sneaks out to touch part of the circle's curve. Turns back to us and whispers. Is it possible he says *"Well, it is impossible to get lost!"* Dear Rilke, without moving from his spot, calls out *"You do not need to go forward to it, but only to go back"*.[47] Several unnamed mothers stand around giggling; a small girl plays with her bangle. It is pointless to keep describing personal reactions. The thing is the thing is. And chaos limps off, momentarily with less, while God promises to return the gold (with interest!).

The World's Yard

Right at the back of the world's yard I am sitting. The most collaborative things I can see are rocks. They are also quite urgent and have dropped the need to dress up like dead people. Near them is a rhinoceros drinking whiskey. An evolution man stands nearby and gestures as if he wants to join the party. The executioners peer through the lot of us and suggest what we might need is a religious polish. Just then I spot a very goodlooking god who has come alone.

The God of Things

The God of Things likes stuff. He understands that
everyone is robbed and cheated. He points out this and that
and the other. I pour us both vodka and propose the toast:
"This is what happens when you'd rather taste heaven in
hell than hell in heaven." And the God of Things raises
his glass and tosses it down. He likes stuff. He coughs and
wipes his hand across his mouth. "The thing is!" he says,
"because there are examples of things which do not exist."

The World's Yard

Right at the back of the world's yard I am sitting. Moon turning pale, ambushed by dawn. One devoted star perfecting faith so that the sky opens around it like a hundred children shouting in a game. So the day begins, disturbing the stream and the perfect mountain over there. Climbing my mind its peak declares "God's infinite distance from mankind".[48] "Then these words [from a calling crow]: *'Suppressing distance kills. The gods die only in our midst.'* "[49]

Under God

God uses a dildo[50] in order to be all things to all people.
God is the bridge, the umbrella, the sky. God is the stump,
the wall, the wound. God rests on us as a frame collapsed.
Crushed under God we sob, we gasp, we scream. God uses a
dildo for pleasure and pain. All things to all people.[51]

The World's Yard

Right at the back of the world's yard I am sitting. Feet buried in the cool grass of Spring. Near me a man erects a glass tent that a field of dust immediately crawls inside. The wind is red because it is Autumn. Everything is dying. Call it a graveyard and water the flowers. Winter's frost is all through the heart's brutal orchard. I have been sitting here all Summer watching the snakes shake their skins. Above the calendar time arches. Now happened a long time ago.

Where is My Soul?

I left myself. Leaving myself is like giving God back the permission he gave me. Its absence uses me to end with.

The World's Yard

Right at the back of the world's yard I am sitting. The original shadow is falling across the landscape. In its swiftness I vow, in honour of eternity, to spend the next five minutes with you. Your face is stark. Seeing you is like a jolt. I might have tripped over you or run into you. You cast a shade of your own. It reaches right over there, to the yard next door where I see someone sitting. As your darkness creeps, today comes undone in their hands. Gently.

The Divine Presence

The divine presence has to happen for the first time. (Rilke finding he's the first poet to live without it.) An ordeal the type of which is usually determined by your social status. Torture, testimony, the secret always out of reach, the touchstone. The judge? And everyone else. Stuck in their "Habits of being"[52], *living* all over the place. And then! The divine presence. You giggle. The dark spot in the crystal efficiently appearing and offering such prolongation. *Virtu* rare and curious! Speak and you describe yearning. Breathe and your lungs fill with dogged stars. Lift foot and the world spins. Bedspread, dressing table and mat, missing. The loss all over you like the sign of something definite. It was in the grass and no-one had ever seen it before. It was the trail of lovers falling away like a line of ducklings behind the mother's back. It was the mysterious production of writing on a covered slate. And now, this dance, and your heart gets dirty and a grain of sand fills everything! Fascination unravelling in your entrails; the veil, inescapable and unfocussed, withdrawing in the retina to penetrate what was hitherto identikit. Hah! The vacuum is denied by your every action. You know what it is like to be someone else.

The World's Yard

Right at the back of the world's yard I am sitting. Wisdom's painful birth is taking place in two merging hearts. Maelstrom of underneath. The god of fear and precision, precisely and fearlessly, throttles the swallow and occasionally spits out a morsel of terror. These bait our lives. Sniffing around we all share death. (We are creepy reminders of the infinite.) We love the wolves. They chew the casing off the day. (Or should we say rather, *the present.*)

The God that Fights

Shrine-bent and wrapped in fists we have just crawled away from the god that fights.[55] We are like those soldiers, idle warriors, bored in the war, who lay down their weapons and leave for the seaside. Swimming out, they turn their heads to the volcano's shore where the little pigeon brings the church for the flock's small comfort. Turning side to side, seeing with only one eye at a time, they wrest from the water's cool dark a meditative grace. We move with them, forever away from the horizon behind, the topline of god's credenza laid with those he will make a meal of. They pray. We dog-paddle. We *are* all defenceless, yet like the supernatural agents in a poem, our prayers and reaching unfold without victims.

The World's Yard

Right at the back of the world's yard I am sitting. A brown hawk wheels through the barking of three dogs. They are speaking to an orange tractor which replies in baritone to an ocean-storm arguing with the horizon. Quietly, so as not to attract the attention of an envious bolt of lightning, the trunk of a growing pine splits itself into three. Somewhere, a religion is born. Overhead, the sky is secretly bilingual. Day and night.

One in the Hand

Some people think that God is watching them in the
shower. While I'm in the shower I ponder (but I never
sing). I muse that prior to explaining how angels fly,
secular science might explain angels. I hear a rustling and
peering out my holy window, wonder if I'm being stared at
compassionately. But God is gone, not hiding in the bushes.
A small bird warbles there about one in the hand.

The World's Yard

Right at the back of the world's yard I am sitting. Already there is a new mountain on the horizon and coming over it, soldiers. The world is pushed into a corner to make people disappear. Chaos is delighted by a free hand. The children close their eyes to the bodies of the dead rising up in a miracle of temptation. Someone like us walks through with our passions, all the wine and cake more ruined than ever. The shadows are perfect says the sun.

Angels

In their matchless kingdom the angels breed like rabbits.
Depth-rabbits! They rake leaves the colour of ash and
eating plums mix their veins with the cry of the fruit. If
they drink from a fountain bound to earth they turn to
stone over the thirsty tomb. But they aren't coming for you.
Angels unhunt. They are merely a little bit of excitement
around the zero. The first symptom of God.

The World's Yard

Right at the back of the world's yard I am sitting. On the earth's ceiling the light bulb shatters and a child invents fear of the dark. Looking around in the blackness I discover everything is the same distance apart. Over a loudspeaker comes the message that the universe is framed impartially for an endless succession of anonymous plaintiffs and defendants. Then the law arrives and we are all blinded by the lack of illumination.

The House of the World

Leave the house of the world. It is falling down. It is standing. It is always falling down. And standing. It is surrounded by a warm cement wall of lizards. A blessing because lizards spend the day in prayer. Prayer to the perfectly white sky the sun has made for itself in which to hide and ache. To hide in the shade as it straddles the afternoon. It says, Have you heard the cries of the lonely pears or the train's long sound unfurling like a winding sheet for the cold pale day? It says, Have you seen the men who rise at five and stumble out to the edge of their women's cries? Fear the wind, welcome the wind. It blows down the house of the world. It blows open the gate. Do you hear the gate? The gate smiles as I enter. The gate smiles as you leave.

The World's Yard

Right at the back of the world's yard I am sitting. I observe the house in the distance and note that the ladder is not resting in its original position. This is perhaps because the roof has collapsed and the walls are grasping at each other for support. The ladder is not complicated (like a rope swinging from heaven) and its beginning and end are now pointless. Only the rungs are still open to interpretation. I call out that they might want to get off it and go home.

God is Waiting

Left to be vile and despicable all by ourselves, at least we can be secure with the knowledge that God is waiting. In glorious madness. (Or so madly we think of his glory.) We feel confident. Enough to doubt God's existence in the mass of time on our hands. Enough to believe in chance which we despise because it doesn't exist and when it presents itself we are furious. We *are* furious. Furiously we squeeze out life in the peaceful days of death. Furiously we exchange the warm skin of today for a little bit of tomorrow. Furiously we sift through each other for traces of buoyancy. We do so want to stay afloat. At least until God comes—for we know that God is waiting. With what do we pass our lives? Some people hit each other. Others put plums in trays being careful not to bruise the flesh. Some think privately, others figure out things on street corners as if the world was responsible for their urge to describe tics. And that might be. That might be. God hasn't arrived yet to either confirm or deny it. It's all a bit stressful— this sitting around wondering. This being forced to wait "in the second place" as it were. There was a person who was even driven to ask *What is the core of a human being?* Silly enough but they dropped a bomb on one to try and find out! In the last resort, when one is forced, violence will always find an answer of one sort or another. And it is the right of us all to wait for God in a manner that will bear explanation to God when God comes. We make notes for this: "a ladder is a series of steps used to ascend to or descend from heights"; "a glass of water is see-through to a certain extent"; "the horse is sometimes ridden on"; "what makes for a good seat is something soft on top of something hard". We are working on our very own *Codex of Things to Tell God* beginning with how long we have been kept waiting because of the secret of divinity and including somewhere in there the part played by the human mind. We tap the tabletop with our fingers—*plonk plonk plonk*. Occasionally we hear what might be the echo of this sound. Occasionally we find something to do with ourselves in which waiting plays no part.

Acknowledgements

Amethyst Review (UK); *Australian Book Review; Bareknuckle Poet Annual Anthology Vol 001, 2015* (Brentley Frazer & A.G. Pettet, editors, Bareknuckle Books, 2015); *Best Australian Poems 2016* (Sarah Holland-Batt, editor, Black Inc., 2016); *Bloodsongs; dispatches from the poetry wars* (USA); *Bluepepper; Elimae* (USA); *Horseless Review* (USA); *Intercapillary Space* (UK); *Leviathan Quarterly* (UK); *Mad Hatter's Review* (USA); *Nuovi Argomenti* (Italy); *Rabbit; Stride* (UK); *The Last Bohemian;* and *The Manhattan Review* (USA).

'Sitting Worldside' and an earlier version of 'Sleepspot' were included in a series under the title, *Soulchat*, which was shortlisted for the Blake Poetry Prize, 2014.

Epigraph courtesy of Bernhard Grossfeld, from a pre-publication version of "Comparative Legal Semiotics: Numbers in Law", *South African Law Journal*, 2001.

Dedications

'Basic Overview About Approaching Form' is for David Buchbinder.
'The Boneheap' is dedicated to René Char.
'The World's Yard' (p35) is for Peter Boyle.
'God is Waiting' is dedicated to Henri Michaux.
Thanks to David Musgrave for publishing this version of God.
Spoiler: 'The Baby Jesus' is Tim Cronin.

Endnotes

1   Help yourself and Heaven will help you.

2   See Wallace Steven's "Mr. Burnshaw and the Statue", (from *Owl's Clover*), *Opus Posthumous: Poems, Plays, Prose*, (Revised, Enlarged, and Corrected Edition, edited by Milton J Bates), Vintage Books, New York, 1990, p80.

3   Barbara Wright in her "Notes for the 1981 American paperback edition" of Raymond Queneau, *Exercises in Style*, (translated by Barbara Wright), New Directions, New York, 1981 (1947), p3.

4   But hyphenated as in my title to this piece. René Char, "Leaves of Hypnos" [#146], from *Furor and Mystery & Other Writings*, (translated & edited by Mary Ann Caws and Nancy Kline), Black Widow Press, Boston, MA, 2010, p183. The phrase is translated by Mark Hutchinson as "the-husband-who-was-hiding-God", perhaps more of a "game" and note the proper noun—perchance a game with greater potential consequences?? (*Hypnos*, Seagull Books, London, New York, Calcutta, 2014, p41).

5   Or did the cloud say: *I only sense my own movement in the bird's head as it dips?*

6   Fernando Pessoa, *The Book of Disquiet, Composed by Bernardo Soares, Assistant Bookkeeper in the City of Lisbon*, (translated by Alfred Mac Adam), Exact Change, Boston, 1998, pp137-138 & p52. "But I considered that Humanity, being a mere biological idea, and not signifying more than the human animal species, was no more worthy of adoration than any other species of animal. This cult of Humanity, with its rites of Liberty and Equality, always seemed to me a revival of the ancient cults in which animals were like gods or the gods had animal heads." "There are those God himself exploits, the prophets and saints in the emptiness of the world."

7   Claudel on God: "All the things He has created ... are simultaneously necessary to each other." Quoted in Simone de Beauvoir, *The Second Sex*, (translated by H M Parshley), Penguin Books, Harmondsworth, Middlesex, England, 1972 (1949), p255.

8   Barbara Wright, *op cit*, pp5-6.

9   Ikkyu, *Crow with No Mouth*, (versions by Stephen Berg), Copper Canyon Press, Port Townsend, Washington, 1989, 2000, p20.

10   A butchery of Georges Bataille, "I Place my Cock ... ", *The Collected Poems of Georges Bataille* (translated by Mark Spitzer), Dufour Editions, Chester Springs, 1999, p6.

11   Paraphrasing Ezra Pound, "Doria", *Collected Early Poems of Ezra Pound*, New Directions Books, New York, 1976, p193.

12   Edmond Jabès, "The Book of Yukel", *The Book of Questions, Volume 1* (translated by Rosmarie Waldrop), Wesleyan University Press, University Press of New England, Hanover and London, 1991, p292.

13   Fernando Pessoa, *op cit*, p137.

14 The stars my camp, God my lamp.

15 Michael Taussig, *Shamanism, Colonialism, and the Wild Man ~ A Study in Terror and Healing*, The University of Chicago Press, Chicago, London, 1987, p336.

16 Voltaire, "Idole, idolatre, idolatrie; Idol, idolator, idolatry", *Philosophical Dictionary*, (translated & edited by Theodore Besterman), Penguin Classics, Harmondsworth, Middlesex, England, 1971, pp228-229.

17 God gives us permission. We sell it.

18 Hafiz, "The Theater of Freedom", *The Subject Tonight is Love—60 Wild and Sweet Poems of Hafiz*, (translated by Daniel Ladinsky), Penguin Compass, New York, 1996, 2003, p21.

19 *Ibid.*

20 *Ibid.*

21 Elaine Scarry, *The Body in Pain, The Making and Unmaking of the World*, Oxford University Press, New York, Oxford, 1985, p213. As well as this phrase, this whole paragraph owes a debt to Scarry, as does the title of this poem.

22 Paraphrasing Hafiz, "Among Strong Men", *op cit*, p25: "Forget about the common reason, Hafiz, for the only/Enslaves—there is something holy deep inside/Of you that is so ardent and awake//That needs to lie down naked/Next to/God".

23 César Vallejo, "Retable", *The Black Heralds & Other Early Poems*, (edited & translated by Michael Smith and Valentino Gianuzzi), Shearsman Books, Exeter, UK, 2007, p141.

24 F. Gonzalez-Crussi, *Notes of An Anatomist*, Picador, London, 1985, p58.

25 Vicente Huidobro, "Manifesto Perhaps", *The Selected Poetry of Vicente Huidobro* (edited & with an Introduction by David M Guss), New Directions, New York, 1981, p78.

26 http://gods4suckers.net/archives/2005/08/ (now found at https://www.theonion.com/evangelical-scientists-refute-gravity-with-new-intellig-1819567984): Quoting Dr Ellen Carson, a leading Intelligent Falling expert known for her work with the Kansas Youth Ministry. See also the ECFR, founded in 1987, the world's leading institution of evangelical physics, a branch of physics based on literal interpretation of the Bible.

27 *S.Y. v S.Y.* [Orse W] [1963] p37, p51.

28 Nicholas Davies, "Mama is watching over me", *Woman's Day*, 3 September, 2001, p9.

29 Hafiz, "Forgiveness Is the Cash", *op cit*, p3.

30 Dana Gioia, *Can Poetry Matter? Essays on Poetry and American Culture*, Graywolf Press, Saint Paul, 1992, p12.

31 Rosmarie Waldrop, *Thinking Of Follows*, http://epc.buffalo.edu/authors/waldropr/thinking.html, speaking about, and quoting, the poet, Robert Duncan.

32 Edmond Jabès, *The Book of Questions, Volume II*, (translated by Rosmarie Waldrop), Wesleyan University Press, University Press of New England, Hanover, NH, 1983, 1984, 1991, p219.

33 Which by the time I get inside is cold.

34 Philip Fried, "Nathan Sees the Whole Synagogue", *Quantum Genesis and Other Poems*, Zohar Press, New York, 1997, p61.

35 Sarah Dyer, "Why I Am A Girl (part two)", *Why I Am A Girl*, http://www.houseoffun.com/action/kikizine/k-girl.html.

36 José Lezama Lima, *José Lezama Lima: Selections*, (edited & with an Introduction by Ernesto Livon-Grosman), University of California Press, Berkeley, Los Angeles, London, 2005, p35.

37 Fernando Pessoa, "Salutation to Walt Whitman", *A Little Larger Than the Entire Universe, Selected Poems* (translated by Richard Zenith), Penguin Books, London, England, 2006, p209.

38 Friedrich Nietzsche, "What is Noble?", *Beyond Good and Evil, Prelude to a Philosophy of the Future* (translated & with an Introduction and Commentary by R Hollingdale), Penguin Books, Harmondsworth, Middlesex, England, 1973, p199.

39 *Charles Baudelaire, Intimate Journals* (translated by Christopher Isherwood, with an Introduction by W H Auden), A London Panther, 1969, p29.

40 *Ibid*, p33.

41 Don Paterson, *Best Thought, Worst Thought*, Graywolf Press, Saint Paul, Minnesota, USA, 2008, p79.

42 "It does seem fitting to construe carelessly made, shoddy [gods] as in some way analogues of bullshit. But in what way? Is the resemblance that bullshit itself is invariably produced in a careless or self-indulgent manner, that it is never finely crafted, that in the making of it there is never the meticulously attentive concern to detail to which Longfellow alludes? [In the elder days of art/Builders wrought with greatest care/Each minute and unseen part,/For the Gods are everywhere.] Is the bullshitter by his very nature a mindless slob? Is his product necessarily messy or undefined?" This quotation, in which I have replaced his word "goods" with "gods", is taken from Harry G Frankfurt, *On Bullshit*, Princeton University Press, Princeton, New Jersey, 2005, p21.

43 " ... a triangle, for instance, is like God: no one has ever seen it, though crude man-made approximations of it are commonplace." Felipe Fernandez-Armesto, *Truth: A History and a Guide for the Perplexed*, Black Swan, London, 1998 (1997), p98.

44 This piece was inspired by C K Williams' essay, "Beginnings", from C K Williams, *Poetry and Consciousness*, University of Michigan Press, Ann Arbor, 1998, p79, where he speaks of being held down as a child by a school friend and slapped until he admitted such.

45 Bernhard Grossfeld, "Comparative Legal Semiotics: Numbers in Law",

Otto Sandrock and Bernhard Grossfeld (eds), *Rechtsvergleichung fuer die Zukunft*, Muenster, 2005, p39, speaking of the words in the image, "deus geometra" of the French-Lorraine "bible moralisé" (from about 1215, now in the Bodleyan Library in Oxford). Grossfeld's source for it was a reprinted picture in Benoit B Mandelbrot, *The Fractal Geometry of Nature*, New York, New York, 1977 and states "*Mandelbrot* loosely translates the French text on top of the picture: 'Here God creates circles, waves, and fractals'." (Footnote 9, p39.)

46　Friedrich Nietzsche, "Maxims and Interludes", *op cit*, p84.

47　A butchery of a phrase of Rilke's (speaking of dying), "he did not need to go forward to it, but only to go back". Rainer Maria Rilke, "Note-book Entry", *Rodin and Other Prose Pieces*, (translated by C Craig Houstton, with an Introduction by William Tucker), Quartet Books Limited, London, 1986, p115.

48　John Fleming, Hugh Honour and Nikolaus Pevsner, *The Penguin Dictionary of Architecture*, Penguin Books, Harmondsworth, Middlesex, England, 1966, 1972, p102.

49　René Char, (from *The Brittle Age*) quoted by Maurice Blanchot, "The Fragment Word", *The Infinite Conversation* (translated by Susan Hanson), University of Minnesota Press, Minneapolis and London, 1993 (1969), pp309–310. Another rendition of these lines of Char's: "To abolish distance kills. The gods only die by being among us." (*The Brittle Age and Returning Upland*, translated by Gustaf Sobin, Counterpath Press, Denver, 2009, p59.)

50　God's dildo is shaped not like a penis but like a giant finger.

51　For those who would argue that "pleasure and pain" do not constitute "all things to all people", you obviously have not experienced nothingness.

52　After bell hooks, and see Margaret Whitford, *Luce Irigiray: Philosophy in the Feminine*, Routledge, London, 1991.

53　René Char, "Lascaux (IV Young Horse with a Mane of Vapor)", *The Word as Archipelago*, (translated by Robert Baker), Omnidawn Publishing, Richmond, California, 2012, p45 (full line: "The god that fights, the grace that meditates."). For Nancy Kline, "Warrior idol, meditative grace." *Furor and Mystery & Other Writings, op cit*, p359.

200

www.ingramcontent.com/pod-product-compliance
Lightning Source LLC
Chambersburg PA
CBHW030827090426
42737CB00009B/903